jim brickman destiny

5 part of my heart
11 bittersweet
16 meant to be
22 rendezvous
29 hush i'l baby
crooked river
41 crossroads
46 love of my life
50 freedom
56 by chance
61 remembrance
66 your love
71 dest ny
77 what we believe in

Photography by Sandra Johnson

Album Art © 1999 Windham Hill Records

ISBN 978-0-634-00283-0

HAL•LEONARD®
CORPORATION
7777 W. BLUEMOUND RD. P.O. BOX 13819 MILWAUKEE, WI 53213

Visit Hal Leonard Online at
www.halleonard.com

Part of My Heart

By JIM BRICKMAN

Bittersweet

By JIM BRICKMAN

Moderately slow, with expression

mf

With pedal

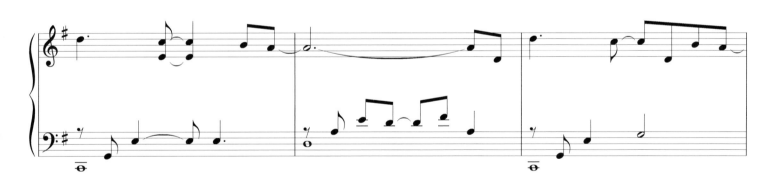

Meant to Be

By JIM BRICKMAN

Moderately slow

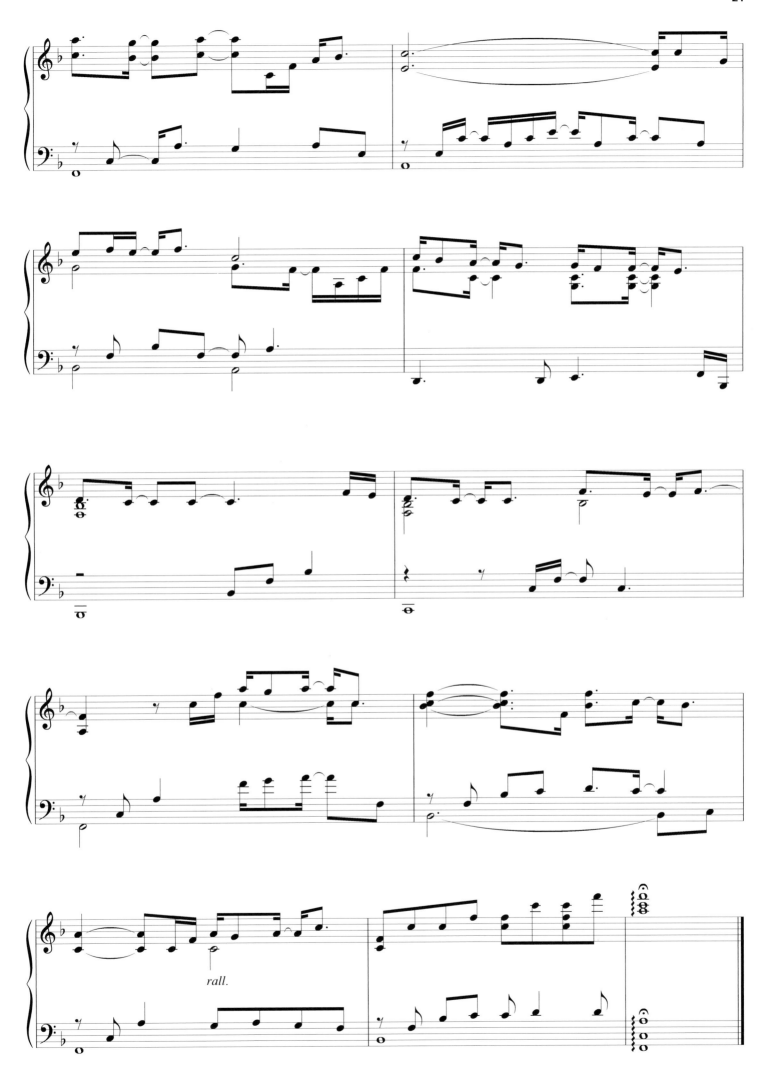

Rendezvous

By JIM BRICKMAN
and BRUCE UPCHURCH

Moderately

With pedal

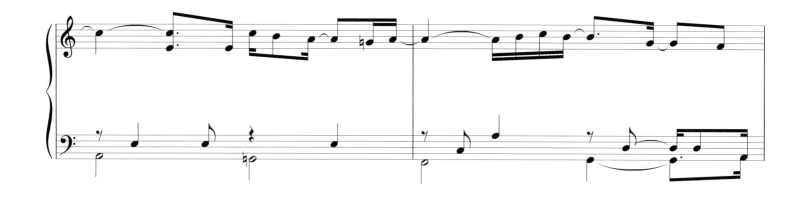

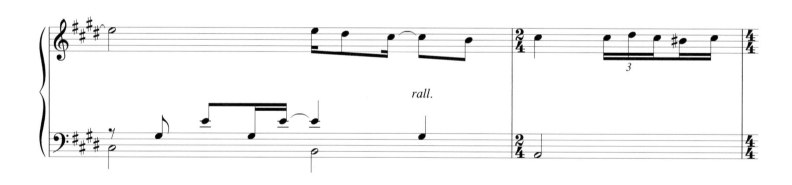

Hush Li'l Baby

Traditional
Arranged by JIM BRICKMAN

* Hush, my lit-tle ba-by, don't __ say __ a word, __

Ma-ma's gon-na buy you a mock-ing-bird. __

* Melody is written an octave higher than sung.

Crooked River

By JIM BRICKMAN

a tempo

Crossroads

By JIM BRICKMAN

Moderately

With pedal

Love of My Life

Words and Music by JIM BRICKMAN
and TOM DOUGLAS

Freedom

By JIM BRICKMAN

Slowly

By Chance

By JIM BRICKMAN

Moderately slow

Remembrance

By JIM BRICKMAN

Your Love

Words and Music by JIM BRICKMAN,
SEAN HOSEIN and DANE DEVILLER

But I could-n't ask __ for more _____ 'cause your love is the great - est gift __ of __ all.

So you could give __ me wings __ to fly, _____ and catch me if ___ I fall. __

Destiny

Words and Music by JIM BRICKMAN,
SEAN HOSEIN and DANE DEVILLER

Original key: D-flat major. This edition has been transposed down one half-step to be more playable.
* Male vocal written at pitch.

What We Believe In

Words and Music by JIM BRICKMAN
and TOM DOUGLAS

D.S. al Coda